Scholastic Canada Biographies

CANADIAN ARTISTS

Maxine Trottier

illustrated by

Tony Meers

Scholastic Canada Ltd.
Toronto New York London Auckland Sydney
Mexico City New Delhi Hong Kong Buenos Aires

Photo Credits

Page 5: Cornelius Krieghoff, *Habitants*, Library and Archives Canada C-011224
Page 7: Cornelius Krieghoff, *Indian Family in the Forest*, The Montreal Museum of Fine Arts,
Miss Mary Fry Dawson Bequest
Page 9: (upper) Library and Archives Canada C-007571; (lower) Cornelius Krieghoff, Canadian 1815-1872,
The Blacksmith's Shop 1871, oil on canvas, 56.5 x 92.1 cm, Art Gallery Of Ontario, Toronto,
gift of Mrs. J. H. Mitchell, Toronto, in memory of her mother, Margaret Lewis Gooderham, 1951
Page 13: British Columbia Archives H-028113
Page 15: Emily Carr (Canadian 1871-1945), *Yan, Q.C.I.*, oil on canvas, Art Gallery of Hamilton,
Gift of Roy G. Cole, 1992
Page 16: (left) © Canada Post Corporation. Reproduced with permission.; (right) British Columbia Archives
D-06009
Page 17: British Columbia Archives B-09610
Page 18: Emily Carr, *Odds and Ends*, Library and Archives Canada NLC-4285
Page 19: Emily Carr, *Shoreline* 1936, oil on canvas, 68.0 x 111.5 cm, McMichael Canadian Art Collection,
gift of Mrs. H. P. de Pencier, 1966.21
Page 22: Tom Thomson as a graphic artist at Grip Limited; J. E. H. MacDonald seen in background at end
of row, [ca. 1911] (Archives of Ontario, F 1066-6. I0010310)
Page 23: (upper) Thomas John Thomson, (1877-1917), *Wild Flowers* (1915), oil on composite wood-pulp boar
21 x 26 cm, Collection of Tom Thomson Memorial Art Gallery, Owen Sound, gift of Louise (Thomson) Henry,
sister of Tom Thomson; (lower) Thomas John Thomson, (1877-1917), *Woods in Winter* (1917),
oil on wood, 13 x 18 cm, Collection of Tom Thomson Memorial Art Gallery, Owen Sound, gift of
Louise (Thomson) Henry, sister of Tom Thomson
Page 25: Tom Thomson studio (exterior), Toronto, 1942, (Archives of Ontario, F 1066-6. I0010308)
Page 27: Tom Thomson fishing, [between 1910 and 1917] (Archives of Ontario, F 1066-6. I0010312
Page 28: Tom Thomson (Canadian 1877-1917), *The Birch Grove, Autumn*, 1915-16, oil on canvas, Art Gallery
of Hamilton, gift of Roy G. Cole, in memory of his parents, Matthew and Annie Bell Gilmore Cole, 1967
Page 29: Tom Thomson, Canadian 1877-1917, *The West Wind* 1916/1917, oil on canvas, 120.7 x 137.9 cm,
Art Gallery Of Ontario, Toronto, gift of the Canadian Club of Toronto, 1926
Page 33: Alexander Colville, *Tragic Landscape*, AN19710261-2126, Beaverbrook Collection of War Art,
© Canadian War Museum (CWM)
Page 35: © Canada Post Corporation. Reproduced with permission; (coins) Royal Canadian Mint, Library and
Archives Canada PA-185468
Page 36: Alex Colville, *Horse and Train*, 1954, glazed tempera on board, collection: Art Gallery of Hamilton,
gift of Dominion Foundries and Steel Ltd., 1957, Copyright A.C. Fine Art Inc.
Page 37: Alex Colville, *Observer*, acrylic polymer emulsion on hardboard, collection of Ron Joyce, Port Hope,
Ontario. Copyright A. C. Fine Art Inc.; (lower) Courtesy Mount Allison University
Page 43: (upper) B. Korda, Library and Archives Canada PA-118724; (lower) Kenojuak Ashevak, *Woman with
Her Dog*, Kenji Photo Design, reproduced with permission of the West Baffin Eskimo Co-operative Ltd.,
Cape Dorset, Nunavut
Page 44: (lower) Judith Eglington, Library and Archives Canada PA-140297
Page 45: (upper) © Canada Post Corporation. Reproduced with permission; (lower) Kenojuak Ashevak,
Ravens' Chorus stonecut, 2002, reproduced with the permission of the West Baffin Eskimo Co-operative Ltd.
Cape Dorset, Nunavut
Page 46: Kenojuak Ashevak, *Shoreline Sentinel*, lithograph, 2003, reproduced with permission of the
West Baffin Eskimo Co-operative Ltd., Cape Dorset, Nunavut

Library and Archives Canada Cataloguing in Publication

Trottier, Maxine

Canadian artists / Maxine Trottier ; illustrated by Tony Meers.

(Scholastic Canada biographies) ISBN 0-439-95756-7

1. Artists—Canada—Biography—Juvenile literature. 2. Art, Canadian—Juvenile literature.
I. Meers, Tony II. Title. III. Series.

NX513.Z8T76 2005   j709'.2'271   C2005-900598-X

ISBN-10 0-439-95756-7 / ISBN-13 978-0-439-95756-4

Mixed Sources
Product group from well-managed
forests and other controlled sources
www.fsc.org Cert no. SGS-COC-003098
© 1996 Forest Stewardship Council
FSC

For Bill, whose presence in my life is a work of art.
— M.T.

Contents

Cornelius Krieghoff

Celebrating Life in Quebec

Cornelius David Krieghoff was born in the city of Amsterdam in the Netherlands on June 19, 1815. He was the third of four children. By 1820 his German father, Johann, and Flemish mother, Isabella, had moved the family to Düsseldorf, Germany. Two years later, the Krieghoffs were living in the Bavarian city of Schweinfurt, where Cornelius's father ran a wallpaper manufacturing business. It was set up in the common hall of a 12th century castle, where the family also had an apartment.

Cornelius learned to play musical instruments. One of his friends wrote that he "used to play and compose music for hours every day." Although he received no formal training, Cornelius was also a talented artist. By the age of 18, he was touring Europe with his mandolin and sketchbook, supporting himself by giving drawing and music lessons.

In 1836 Cornelius Krieghoff immigrated to the United States. There he met Émilie Gauthier, a 15-year-old girl from Boucherville, Quebec, who was working in New York as a servant. The next year, having promised to stay in touch with her, he enlisted in the American army, giving his occupation as "clerk." The military records describe him as having fair hair, a red complexion and being 5 feet 10 ½ inches (about 1.8 metres) tall. He was assigned to Battery 1, 1st United States Artillery, and sent to Florida. There the Seminole people were resisting the U.S. Army, because they were being uprooted to make room for settlers. Cornelius was an artificer, a soldier who maintained the cannons. Three years later he was discharged at Burlington, Vermont, and moved on to Boucherville, Quebec, where he rejoined Émilie and married her.

They settled down and Cornelius took up his art again. A son, Henry, was born. Henry's death in 1841, at only one year old, was a blow to the Krieghoffs. There were other difficulties, since

Habitants, an 1852 watercolour by Krieghoff

Cornelius was unable to make a living with his art. Not only were daguerreotypes – an early kind of photograph – very popular, but Montreal society only cared about art from Europe. The Krieghoffs moved to Buffalo, New York, then to Toronto, Ontario, and finally to Rochester, New York, where Cornelius did have a successful art show. But Émilie was homesick, and so the couple settled at Longueuil, Quebec, and Cornelius set up a studio in Montreal.

He began to make friends among the *habitants*, or French settlers. Wearing a velvet suit and a beaver hat, he watched them as they drove their sleighs, drank in the taverns, ploughed their fields and did chores. He decided to paint the everyday activities that he saw around him. This is known as genre painting, and his lighthearted approach was well-suited to country life. He also hiked out into the countryside to paint the Iroquois at their village at Caughnawaga on the south bank of the St. Lawrence River.

When a subject pleased him, Krieghoff would paint many versions of it. There are about 30 different paintings of him and his friends riding home from a party in a sleigh, dashing past the village gatekeeper without paying the toll.

But the paintings weren't popular with the art collectors in Montreal. Krieghoff could only sell them for $5 and $10 apiece to British army officers or to engineers building a railroad there. He had some small successes in 1847 when his art was

displayed in both Montreal and Toronto. A newspaper review of his work in *La Minerve*, a Montreal newspaper, described one painting, *An Officer's Room in Montreal*, as having "great soundness and transparency of colouring." And that same year Lord Elgin, Canada's Governor General, visited his studio and found his art delightful. Still, Krieghoff sometimes had to work as a sign painter or house painter to support his family.

In 1851 Cornelius Krieghoff met John Budden, an art auctioneer who would change his career. Budden offered to share his home with the Krieghoffs if Cornelius would move his wife and young daughter, Emily, to Quebec City. Two years later, British officers stationed at the Citadel there were buying his paintings to send home to England.

Indian Family in the Forest, oil on canvas by Krieghoff, 1851

With the money he was earning, in 1854 he was able to visit Europe.

Krieghoff returned to Quebec, where his works continued to sell. In the 1860s he spent several years in Europe, painting Canadian scenes from memory. When his health declined, he went to live with Emily and her second husband in Chicago, U.S.A. Although he returned to Quebec in 1870, it was in Chicago that he died in March 1872.

Cornelius Krieghoff's art was not appreciated until long after his death. During his lifetime, some felt that his images of the habitants as fun-loving people, showing parties, celebrations and tipsy men slipping on ice, was undignified. However, today paintings such as *Merrymaking* are part of our country's national heritage, and Krieghoff is considered by many to be the father of Canadian painting. Through his keen eye and detailed technique, he has left us with a lively look at Canada in the 19th century.

(upper) A photograph of Krieghoff, taken between 1850 and 1872 in Quebec City; (lower) *The Blacksmith's Shop*, oil on canvas by Krieghoff, 1871
In 1972, this became a stamp to commemorate the centennial of Krieghoff's death.

Emily Carr

Honouring Trees and Totem Poles

1871 was an important year for British Columbia. It joined Confederation and became the sixth Canadian province – and Emily Carr was born.

The youngest of five sisters, Emily arrived on a cold December night. Her mother, Emily, and father, Richard – a prosperous grocer – were British immigrants. Their large house in Victoria was surrounded by English-style gardens where little "Millie" used to play.

Millie showed an early talent for drawing. One day, she took a burned stick from the hearth and sketched their dog, Carlow, on a brown paper bag. Years later, the bag would be found among her

father's papers. On it he had written, "By Emily, aged eight." Recognizing her ability, he arranged art lessons for her.

Before Emily was 17, both of her parents died. She finished her year of high school but didn't go back. Instead, she enrolled in a local art school. When she asked to travel to Europe with friends to study art, her sisters refused. She was given permission by their guardian to study in California. Emily wasn't pleased with her progress and later wrote, "The type of work I brought home from San Francisco was humdrum."

In 1893 Emily returned to Victoria and gave art lessons to children at her home. Her sisters disliked

Emily Carr at age 21 or 22

the mess and noise, so Emily turned the family barn into a teaching studio. The next year she had her first exhibition at the Victoria Fall Fair. Each painting was signed M. Emily Carr.

In 1899 Emily sailed with her sister Lizzie to the west coast of Vancouver Island. They visited the mission on the Nootka Reserve in Ucluelet. The Nootka people let Emily sketch them and their houses. Finding the hand gestures she used to communicate amusing, they gave her the name *Klee Wyck*, which means "laughing one."

At the end of that summer, Emily Carr sailed to London, England, to study at the Westminster

School of Art. Unhappy in the city, she moved to Cornwall. She pushed herself until she became ill and spent over a year in a sanatorium. Unable to paint, she raised nests of songbirds in her room.

In 1904 Emily returned to Canada, and three years later she and her sister Alice took a cruise north to Alaska. There Emily saw a display of Haida and Tlingit totem poles. Deeply moved by their beauty and convinced that in time they might disappear, she decided to paint as many as she could during the next years.

By 1910 Emily had saved enough money from various jobs to travel to Paris with Alice. There she felt confined in the airless rooms of the art school, Académie Colarossi, writing that "it was like putting

...an, Q.C.I. (Queen Charlotte Islands), oil on canvas by Emily Carr, 1912

a pine tree in a pot." She went on to take outdoor classes on the French coast. Instead of watercolours, Emily began to paint with oils. She experimented with the Post-Impressionist style, one that allowed her to use bold colours and sweeping brush strokes.

Back in Canada Emily Carr held a show in 1912. Her new style was ridiculed. With her sheepdog, Billie, she travelled the British Columbia coast, visiting remote Native villages. She completed almost 200 works. In April 1913 she rented a hall in Vancouver. She displayed her works and lectured on totem poles. The public response was not good.

Emily Carr's *Big Raven* (oil on canvas, 1931) became a stamp in 1971 to commemorate the 100th anniversary of her birth.

(right) Emily Carr in her studio with one of her paintings behind her

Disappointed, she contacted the B.C. government, but they showed no interest in buying them, saying they were too artistic and didn't show a real picture of Native life.

Crushed and bitter, she returned to Victoria. On family property, Emily built a small apartment building she called The House of All Sorts, hoping it would give her some income and time to paint. Unable to afford help, she did all the work herself.

To survive Emily hooked rugs and made pottery. She raised Old English Sheepdogs and Brussels Griffons. By 1924, she was decorating her pottery with Native designs to sell in a local gift shop. Feeling guilty, she explained, "I did keep the Indian design pure."

In 1927 Eric Brown, the director of the National Gallery of Canada, sent Emily Carr a train ticket, inviting her to participate in a show featuring West Coast art. On the way to Ottawa, the train stopped in Toronto, where she met some of the Group of Seven. Their art made a great impression on her.

The exhibit was a big success. Finally Emily Carr's work was being recognized. She began to take sketching trips, and in 1933 she bought a trailer she named "The Elephant." She cooked and worked outside, since the trailer had barely enough room for herself, her pets and her supplies.

Emily Carr entertains friends at "the Elephant." Her pet monkey is on her shoulder.

Odds and Ends, oil by Emily Carr, circa 1939

18

oreline, oil on canvas by Emily Carr, 1936

Then, at the age of 66, Emily Carr had a heart attack. Less able to travel or paint, she began to write about her life. In 1940 she moved in with her sister Alice, after finding new homes for many of her pets. Her book *Klee Wyck* won the Governor General's Award in 1941. In time seven more books were published. Emily died on March 2, 1945.

Emily Carr is one of Canada's most admired artists. Her work is known for its swirling energy and use of light, and her story is one of true determination. Through her art, the love she had for the land and people of the Pacific Northwest lives on.

Tom Thomson
Glorifying the Woodlands

Tom Thomson came into the world on August 5, 1877, at Claremont, Ontario. Two months later his parents, Margaret and John, moved with their six children to Rose Hill Farm, near the town of Leith on Georgian Bay. There, four more children were born. Tom enjoyed drama, played the mandolin and was a violinist in the school orchestra. His health was not good, though, so his parents took him out of school. Tom loved the outdoors. When not helping on the farm, he fished or hiked around Georgian Bay.

From the time Tom was 21 until he was 30, he searched for a career. He worked as an apprentice machinist in the nearby city of Owen Sound. He went to business school in Chatham, Ontario, and then in Seattle, Washington, where two of his older brothers had moved. In Seattle he found work with first one engraving company, then another. It was during this time that he began doing nature sketches in crayon and watercolour.

By 1904 Tom was back in Owen Sound. The next year he moved to Toronto and worked as a senior artist for Legg Brothers Photoengraving Company. He was paid $11 a week. He began to take art lessons.

It was a job move in 1907 to Grip Limited in Toronto, a business that designed advertisements and posters, which opened the door for him. It was

This photograph shows Tom Thomson working as a graphic artist at Grip Limited in 1911. J. E. H. MacDonald is seated at the end of the row.

Wild Flowers, oil sketch by Tom Thomson, 1915

Woods in Winter, oil sketch by Tom Thomson, 1917

there that he met J. E. H. MacDonald, who was the head designer. Tom worked alongside Franklin Carmichael, Arthur Lismer, Frederick Varley and Frank Johnston. These men, along with Lawren Harris and A. Y. Jackson, would later form the Group of Seven. The artists had a deep effect on one another, and their unique style began to develop.

Tom bought a good oil sketch box and began working in oils. In May of 1912, he made his first trip to Algonquin Park with a friend from Grip. He fell in love with the park, taking dozens of photographs, but he lost most of his film when the canoe overturned. He returned in July with another artist. This time he lost many of his sketches when their canoe capsized in the rapids. But that fall Tom began to rework some sketches into his first large oil paintings.

It was in 1912 that Dr. James MacCallum, prompted by a friend, tracked down the artist in Toronto. Within two years he was Thomson's patron, supporting and encouraging his talent. With Dr. MacCallum's financial help, Thomson was able to work as a serious artist. MacCallum would later

"The Thomson Shack" in Toronto, as it looked in 1942

explain, "The north country enthralled him . . . He began to paint [to] express the emotions the country inspired in him."

The Toronto art critics did not understand the art of Tom Thomson and his friends. The images weren't realistic enough, so the critics called their style "The Hot Mush School." One night, very frustrated, Thomson threw his brushes and paintbox into the Algonquin bush. He spent most of the next day repairing his box and finding his paints.

Tom Thomson moved into a Toronto studio with A. Y. Jackson. When Jackson went overseas during World War I, Thomson shared the studio with artist Frank Carmichael. Then the studio was

rented out to someone else, and Thomson and Arthur Lismer moved into the tool shed behind it. For this shack, Thomson paid $1 a month in rent. With canoe paddles in the corner, fishing gear hanging on the walls and a small bunk and cast iron cooking stove, it was like an Algonquin cabin.

Needing money, in 1916 Thomson got a job as a fire ranger in Algonquin Park for the summer. Here was a job that would give him a chance to be out in the wilderness he so loved. But it didn't allow him much time for sketching.

He spent the winter in Toronto, entering four paintings in an art show. The next spring he returned to the park – camping in the woods, working as a guide when he could, and finishing one sketch per

Lawren Harris took this photograph of Tom Thomson fishing between 1910 and 1917.

day. He would set out his oil sketches to dry on the trails, picking them up when he returned from hiking. Once, an animal chewed up a painting. Thomson told a friend the animal was an excellent critic.

On July 8 of 1917, Thomson set out to do some fishing with a bit of bread and bacon for bait. That afternoon an upturned canoe was spotted on Canoe Lake. Eight days later, his body was found floating in the water. Tom Thomson was buried the next day in a cemetery overlooking the lake and an inquest

27

The Birch Grove, Autumn, oil on canvas by Tom Thomson, 1915-1916

was held that night. The official verdict was accidental death by drowning. On July 18 Thomson's remains were exhumed and sent to Owen Sound. He was reburied the next day in the Leith Cemetery near the family farm.

To this day a cairn stands at Hayhurst Point on Canoe Lake. Fastened to it is a plaque designed by J. E. H. Macdonald. The inscription begins,

TO THE MEMORY OF TOM THOMSON

ARTIST WOODSMAN AND GUIDE

It remains a tribute to a man who was deeply missed by his fellow artists.

Tom Thomson's career lasted only five years, and yet in that time he left behind hundreds of sketches and paintings of the Canadian wilds. *The West Wind*, believed to be his last painting, has become a symbol of Canada's spirit. If he had lived, there would not have been a Group of Seven. There would have been a Group of Eight.

The West Wind, oil on canvas by Tom Thomson, 1916-1917

Alex Colville

Creating Magic Moments

David Alexander Colville was born in Toronto, Ontario, on August 24, 1920. At the age of seven he moved with his family to St. Catharines, Ontario, where his father, a Scottish immigrant, worked on the locks as a steelworker and riveter.

Two years later Florence and David Colville, Alex's parents, moved the family to Amherst, Nova Scotia, where his father worked as the foreman in a steel plant. Alex was fascinated by the blueprints for the constructions. "I was very good at geometry when I was a kid at school," he has said. "I was fortunate to have very good teachers."

That year he became very ill with pneumonia. During his recovery he spent a great deal of time alone. "I began to read," he recalls, "really for the first time, and did quite a few drawings, simply because I was alone and had to find something to do." When not reading he was drawing machines, cars, planes and boats, as well as making scale models of airplanes that he would sell.

He was 14 when he enrolled in a weekly art class taught by Mrs. Sarah Hart. It was there that he met Stanley Royle, an artist and university professor. Although Alex had plans to study politics and law when he finished high school, it was Royle who urged him to consider art.

In 1938 Alex began to study art at Mount Allison University in Sackville, New Brunswick.

Tragic Landscape, oil on canvas by Alex Colville, 1945

From Royle, who was one of his instructors, he learned that drawing and planning before beginning a painting were very important. Alex adopted this philosophy. Later in his career, he would do as many as 24 sketches to prepare for a single work.

Alex Colville graduated with a degree in fine arts in 1942 and married Rhoda Wright, who would become a frequent model for his art. Because World War II was raging overseas, he enlisted in the army, serving as a war artist from 1944 to 1946. The war had a great influence upon his work. When Germany surrendered, Colville was given an assignment that affected him deeply. He was sent to Bergen-Belsen concentration camp, where he

painted the mass graves in which starved and executed prisoners had been thrown. Today, many of these drawings and paintings are in the Canadian War Museum in Ottawa.

Alex Colville returned to Canada and taught art at Mount Allison for 17 years. He and Rhoda raised three sons and a daughter. In 1963 he decided to devote himself only to painting. He had been working for many years in a distinctive style called magic realism, which shows real things and people, but also contains a suggestion of fantasy or mystery. *Family and Rainstorm*, an ordinary scene of a family getting into the car, set against a threatening sky, is a fine example of this.

Alex Colville's *Family and Rainstorm* (oil, 1955) became a stamp for Canada Day 1982, one of 12 stamps portraying "Canada Through the Eyes of Its Artists."

Centennial coins designed by Alex Colville, 1967

In 1973 Alex Colville and his wife moved to Wolfville, Nova Scotia, into the house Rhoda's father had built and where she had been born. He turned the third floor into a studio and office, where he could sketch and paint. His work continued to be bought and displayed in museums, offices and homes across Canada and around the world.

Canada has showered Alex Colville and his powerful paintings with honours. He designed Canada's 1967 Centennial coins, and that year he was named an Officer of the Order of Canada. He designed the Governor General's Medal in 1978, and was made a Companion of the Order of Canada in 1982. In 2002 his painting, *Church and Horse* was that year's Masterpiece in Canadian Art postage stamp, and he was inducted into Canada's Walk of Fame. The next year he won a Governor General's Award in Visual and Media Arts. He has received many honourary university degrees. And his painting, *Horse and Train*, was even used as an album cover by Canadian singer-songwriter Bruce Cockburn. Colville has said, "What the recognition does is tell me that I wasn't crazy to think I could be an artist."

Most of Alex Colville's work has been inspired by his personal experiences. He is considered to be one of the world's finest magic realist painters. His

Horse and Train, glazed tempera on board by Alex Colville, 1954

Observer, acrylic polymer emulsion on hardboard by Alex Colville, 2002

Alex Colville and his wife with Fine Arts students at Mount Allison University, 2003

art can be found in many collections, including the Museum of Modern Art in New York, the Musée Nationale d'Art Moderne in Paris and the National Gallery of Canada in Ottawa. He has said, "You spend your whole life telling people what it's like to be alive." Over the years his art, with its magical images of the real world, has done exactly that.

Kenojuak
Designing the North

Kenojuak Ashevak is one of Canada's most important artists. She works in a remote community in Nunavut, travelling south for special occasions. Her unique designs are known all over the world. But her road to becoming an artist was a long and difficult one.

On October 3, 1927, an Inuit camp stood at Ikirasak, Cape Dorset, on south Baffin Island. That day at the camp, a baby girl was born. Her father, Usuaqjuk, an Inuit hunter and fur trader, and his wife, Silaqqi, named the baby Kenojuak. One winter when Kenojuak was very young, her father was

murdered by rival hunters at Mansel Island. Silaqqi took her children to her relatives at Sapujjuaq camp. Such were the harsh and difficult beginnings of Kenojuak's life.

Kenojuak was raised by her grandmother, who taught her traditional handicrafts. Her family hunted and trapped, so Kenojuak spent her early years travelling from camp to camp by dogsled in the winter and on foot or by boat in the summer. "In the cold seasons of the year," she recalls, "a *qarmaq* (a winterized tent) served as our housing."

A marriage was arranged for her in 1946. At first she was a reluctant bride. She would toss rocks at her husband, Johnniebo, but in time she came to love him. Their first home was an *iglu* with a window made from a block of ice. "That winter is the only time I recall living in a snowhouse for an entire season," she recalls. While her husband hunted, Kenojuak ran the home as other Inuit women did. She scraped skins with an *ulu*, butchered seals and made clothing.

Kenojuak's first baby, a boy they named Jamasie, was born the next year in the *qarmaq* her husband had built. That summer all the Inuit were ordered to go to Cape Dorset where there was a hospital ship. Everyone was X-rayed and the sick were taken south to hospitals.

With the arrival of a nurse and a teacher in 1950, the Cape Dorset community began to change. The next year James Houston and his wife, Alma, arrived. Houston was not only a government administrator, he was an artist, and interested in helping the Inuit.

The next year the RCMP passed through the camp where Kenojuak was living with the family. She had a daughter as well as a son now, and was expecting another baby. The officers told her that the X-rays taken last summer showed she had tuberculosis. She would have to go south to a sanitarium for treatment. Kenojuak gave birth to a son shortly after. Unable to take him with her, she

gave the baby up for adoption. Not knowing she wouldn't see her family for three and a half years, Kenojuak was flown to the Parc Savard Hospital in Quebec City.

In 1953 she received a terrible letter. Her family had eaten tainted walrus meat, and although Johnniebo was recovering, the children had died. Kenojuak suffered a relapse. Slowly recovering, she did leatherwork, sewing and beadwork when not in bed. In May of 1955, she was cured and able to return home by boat. "When we saw ice floes, we all felt rejuvenated, in spite of suffering from seasickness."

Alma Houston encouraged the Inuit women to make and sell crafts. Kenojuak experimented with sealskin appliqué. She made *kamiit* (boots), wall hangings and soapstone carvings. Then James

Kenojuak (front row, second from left) with other Inuit artists of the Cape Dorset cooperative, August 1961

Woman with Her Dog, sculpture in serpentine by Kenojuak Ashevak, 1988

Houston gave her some paper and pencils and urged her to try drawing. He went on to teach her and other Cape Dorset women how to make prints from their drawings. Kenojuak's first print was titled *Rabbit Eating Seaweed.*

In 1959, with Houston's help, the Inuit of Cape Dorset formed The West Baffin Eskimo Co-operative. Kenojuak's prints began to be seen and appreciated. Three years later, the National Film Board made a film about her called *Eskimo Artist:*

43

Kenojuak with two of her works – *The World Around Me* (above) and *Colourful Sentinel* (below) at Cape Dorset, December 1980

Kenojuak. In it she observed that "a piece of paper from the outside world is as thin as the shell of a snowbird's egg." Though she drew fish and mammals and humans, birds became one of her favourite topics.

Even today Kenojuak does not sketch before she draws. She simply begins a drawing, completes the outlines of the figures, and carefully shades them to create a complex pattern of shape and colour. Once a drawing is finished, Inuit stonecutters create a print using her drawing as the design.

Canada has showered Kenojuak and her work with honours. She was among the first Canadians to receive the Order of Canada in 1967, and was

Kenojuak's *The Enchanted Owl* (1960) became a stamp for the centennial of the Northwest Territories in 1970.

Ravens' Chorus, stonecut by Kenojuak Ashevak, 2002

elected to the Royal Canadian Academy of Arts in 1974. Three of her images have been released as Canadian postage stamps. One stamp, *The Enchanted Owl*, marked the centennial of the Northwest Territories in 1970. Kenojuak was made a

Shoreline Sentinel, lithograph by Kenojuak Ashevak, 2003

Companion of the Order of Canada in 1982, and in 2001 she received a star on Canada's Walk of Fame.

Kenojuak and Johnniebo settled in Cape Dorset in 1966, working together until his death. She still lives there, sharing the proceeds from her art with her extended family. "The Inuit tradition is to help each other," she explains. Her art is simply a part of her life, as is returning to the land to hunt and fish with her family in the summers. Through her magical images, Kenojuak Ashevak is helping to keep alive the culture of the Inuit people of Canada.